IT'S A LAB'S WORLD

IT'S A LAB'S WORLD

An Illustrated Collection of Everything Labrador Retriever

Edited by Jason Smith

WILLOW CREEK PRESS

Published by Willow Creek Press
P.O. Box 147
Minocqua, Wisconsin 54548

Design: Donnie Rubo

Library of Congress Cataloging-in-Publication Data

Smith, Jason A., 1974-
    It's a lab's world : an illustrated collection of everything labrador
retriever / by Jason Smith.
        p. cm.
    ISBN 1-59543-392-9 (hardcover : alk. paper)
    1. Labrador retriever. 2. Labrador retriever--Pictorial works. I. Title.
    SF429.L3S49 2006
    636.752'7--dc22
                                    2006003992

Printed in Canada

Contents

Part 1
Star of the Show

> **The Labrador retriever has been America's favorite dog for so many years now that it's hard to imagine the breed ever relinquishing its position as tops in the land... and in our hearts.**
>
> – D.A. Young

Wrap your mind around this statistic: Since the year 2000, nearly one million Labrador retrievers have been registered with the American Kennel Club (AKC). One million. 1,000,000. Six zeroes. Not only is that one million animals, that's one million dogs. And not only is that one million dogs, that's one million of just one breed of dog. Hold on, let me rephrase that: a million dogs of one breed that were *registered*. How many more are lounging around sofas and front porches without papers or fancy names?

"Labs don't crowd our personal space. We tell them things we'd never share with anyone, at least not with any degree of comfort. They listen and understand."

—E. Donnall Thomas Jr.

The exact number of Labs registered with the AKC in 2000 was 922,920. For 16 consecutive years, the Labrador retriever has been the most popular dog in America, and when you delve into the breed, it's easy to see why. These clowns dressed in black, yellow, or chocolate fur epitomize the very best the world of dogdom has to offer. They are loyal, dedicated, smart, energetic, goofy, people-pleasing, hardworking, lovable, gentle, focused, trainable, and a thousand other good things. Sure, they may shed too much and are too big to hold on your lap while you drive, but some of us don't own dogs for ornamentation. We own a dog to have a D-O-G, and no breed is better at fulfilling the role of "man's best friend" than the Lab.

In the play that is life—with a stage spread across rolling prairies and snow-capped mountains, painted deserts, patchwork farmland, and the big-city lights—mankind may get top billing, but the Labrador retriever steals the show as the star performer. As the most popular dog in America (every year, the number of Labs registered with the AKC are nearly triple the number of the second most popular, the golden retriever), there's a decent chance that when you come across a dog it'll be a Lab. Or at least have a smidgen of Lab in it. These black, yellow, and chocolate superdogs

As one of the most trainable and good-natured dogs, the Lab is an especially good pet for children.

haven't just wormed their way into our society, they've taken it by storm with a pawprint stamp. In so many ways Labs are a part of millions of people's everyday lives—as hunters, service

animals, athletic competitors, and family bums. In the myriad pictures that now comprise the American family, it's not surprising to find a Lab fulfilling the role as the creature without opposable thumbs in the house.

As you'll see in the next part of this book, it almost seems like Labs were bred for people from day one. Their lives are a history of service to humans, and their amazing intelligence, trainability, and apparent genetic affinity for people—both willing to forgive our foibles and always searching for what pleases us—have made humans turn to the Labrador retriever when they want to teach a dog to do something. And in so doing, we've guaranteed them a place among the canine race that they won't surrender anytime soon.

> 66 *I can't ever imagine being*
> *without one or two Labs,*
> *nor do I expect to. I need the*
> *comfort and companionship*
> *they so willingly and amply*
> *provide. I have come to*
> *absolutely depend on it.* 99
>
> – Gene Hill

Breed Standard

Every breed's early development usually occurs because of the dedication of a few individuals focused on creating a dog to suit their needs. And with that dedication comes a careful breeding program that promotes the desired qualities—both physical appearance and mental capabilities—so that they become "fixed" in the bloodline of the dog. As such, there are set "standards" for how an individual dog must look, and the custodian of these standards in the U.S. has been, since 1884, the American Kennel Club (AKC).

The Labrador retriever is found in the AKC's "Sporting Group," which includes the English setter, pointer,

The Labrador retriever is a worker and an athlete, and as such is a member of the AKC's "Sporting Group."

The Lab is an expert water dog and has a characteristic "otter tail," which acts as a rudder when he swims.

golden retriever, and the spaniels (the hounds have their own group). All of these dogs were originally bred for hunting purposes. The AKC is careful to note that dogs in the Sporting Group "require regular, invigorating exercise." Don't say you weren't warned.

Physically, the Lab's form helps it perform its function; its solid build, dense, insulating coat, characteristic "otter tail" (which acts unmistakably like a rudder), eager-to-please temperament, and determination all help the Lab perform as America's premier waterfowl and upland bird hunter and retriever. Everything about them—the way they run, swim, and work (retrieve) —should be smooth and effortless ("without lumber or cloddiness" is how the AKC puts it).

What the world has discovered, though, is that the basic personality of the Lab is so endearing—and so fixed in the breed as to be noted in the standard—that its place in the home and the lives of the family set it apart from the rest of dogdom. How else can you justify 16 consecutive years as the most registered dog?

"Why can't you just hang out the window like other dogs?"

Just because a Lab may not perfectly adhere to the AKC's breed standard, however, doesn't make it any less a Lab. In fact, most Labs couldn't place in an AKC bench (conformation) show, in which dogs earn titles and prizes based on their appearance. The Labrador retriever is one of those breeds that,

because of its popularity, has diverged into different lines with strikingly dissimilar appearances. And proponents of the differing groups can be quite hostile toward one another.

Though the breed standard acknowledges the fact that Labs are primarily hunting dogs and should have a form that allows them to fulfill this role, there is widespread feeling that most Labs seen trotting around Westminster would be hard-pressed to spend a day chasing pheasants or swimming down a duck. Generally speaking, the "show Lab" is shorter, "squattier," not as overall muscular, and broader in the head and snout than the typical "field Lab." Field Labs, generally speaking, are longer in the leg and tail, explosive in their drive,

❝With all that's been said of their winsome ways and their ability to love, we should stop once in a while to remember that there are few creatures on earth as strong, courageous, committed, and just plain tough as a Labrador retriever.❞

– Steve Smith

narrower in the forequarters but deeper in the chest that rises to a leaner belly, and, at first glance, just look like they could go all day in the field. But you'll never find one of these Labs being led around the show ring.

There is a third type of Lab, one
that seems to be more "classic," and it
shouldn't be surprising that this Lab
is the "British Lab," for the breed
found its earliest cultivators in
England. British Labs more closely

If you throw it, he will retrieve it—
over, and over and over again!

resemble what the AKC standard, set long ago and modified last in 1994, sets down as the ideal Lab. Indeed, a British Lab cannot earn a field title without also claiming a show title. Thus, there has been a rise in the popularity of British Labs in the States as people try to get back to what the Lab "should look like and do." (Incidentally, the Lab is also the most popular dog in the United Kingdom.)

In reality, though, it seems that the general population is content to have these three "types" of Labs—the typical show dog, the typical field Dog (often called the American field Lab, or American style), and the British Lab, which best marries both pursuits. It really comes down to what a person or family wants out of their Lab: If field or athletic competition and arduous hunting are in the Lab's future, then the American Lab is probably best. For a life in the show ring, the classic show Lab will work best. For someone who might want to do both or just wants the "classic Lab," the British style of Lab might be in order.

If you just want a lovable family dog, you can't go wrong with any of them. It is absolutely the work of the Divine that in all the breedings for appearance and ability—be it in a ring or a duck marsh—the Lab's personality has remained constant, unwavering, and, if anything, has progressed more toward their love of people. Whether the

Patient and gentle are two great Lab traits.

Three colors, one breed, countless personalities. Pairings of two blacks, black and yellow, black and chocolate, and yellow and chocolate will produce litters with the potential for all colors. Two yellow parents will produce only yellow, and two chocolates will produce only yellow and chocolates.

dog is a show champion, hunter, service dog, drug detector, the chubbiest one you've ever seen, the lankiest long jumper soaring through the air, or anywhere in between, their most treasured place is by mankind's side.

The hallmark of the breed is, undoubtedly, the three colors—yellow, black, and chocolate. (Don't dare call a yellow Lab a "golden" Lab... that's for that "other" breed.) Some Labs may have white spots on the chest or paws, and there can even be some "brindling." While some of these coat color oddities may disqualify that dog from attaining a show title, they don't make the dog any less of a Lab.

How is coat color determined? Genetics. Though the discussion is beyond the scope of this book and is

presented in much more detail in many other volumes about Labs, suffice it to say that there are certain genes that dictate what color a Lab pup will be, and these genes are, of course, inherited from the parents. How these genes combine at the moment that a new pup is formed in the dam determines the dog's color, with black being the dominant color, and chocolate and yellow recessive. Through basic genetics (and without using such words as genotype, phenotype, heterozygous, homozygous, loci, alleles, and chromosomes), it is possible to have a litter of Lab pups with all three colors represented.

No matter what scuttlebutt may be floating around dog circles or the Internet, though, don't believe the hype

about the mental characteristics of the different colors of Labs. It was long believed that black Labs were the most athletic, best hunters, and had the most drive; yellow were the most laid back, intelligent, and the ideal family companions; and chocolates were,

The black color in Labs is the dominant and oldest color, started by the earliest breeders of Labs—Malmesbury, Buccleauch, and Home. The yellow color was cultivated by C.J. Radclyffe, Montagu Guest, Lord Wimborne, and, later, Mrs. Arthur Wormald in the late 1800s and early 1900s. The chocolate color had its biggest support from in Sir Ian Walker and J.G. Severn in the 1930s.

Other Colors?

You might see something other than black, yellow, or chocolate Lab puppies advertised for sale. Some of the other colors that might pop up in litter listings are: white, red, fox-red, or silver. Don't be fooled; these aren't new genetic mutations. Yellow, as the AKC breed standard states, can "range in color from fox-red to light cream"; sometimes, they can be almost white. These are all genetically yellow Labs. By the same token, a "silver Lab" is, genetically, a chocolate Lab. The dusky, silvery color comes from another gene called "dilute," which changes the pigment distribution in the hair follicles so that the chocolate color appears more silver. Black and yellow Labs can also have this feature, which is why some black Labs can be very shiny and others are more dusky or charcoal looking.

well... they didn't fall into either of these groups. Some of the belief in these stereotypes may have had a basis in the fact that, with black being the dominant color, there were simply more black dogs at the time the breed was being developed. As it was being developed, those dogs chosen for breeding were the ones that displayed great potential in the field, both in hunting situations and in early field competitions. Since most of the Labs were black, there was a greater chance of black Labs being in field events and succeeding. In the old "survival of the fittest" mentality, those dogs that were successful were the ones chosen for breeding, meaning that the genes for the dominant coat color—black—were the ones passed down.

> *"Like all teenagers, Labs in their first few seasons display more physical ability than judgement."*
>
> – Tom Davis

But with proponents of the yellow and chocolate colors coming on the scene a little later in the Lab's history and cultivation, those colors, though not as common at the time, also competed and were successful and were chosen for breeding, thus perpetuating those colors.

It is a testament to the breed that no matter the innumerable breedings and crosses and combinations of bloodlines and colors, a Lab is to be judged not by the color of his fur but by the content of his character. Perhaps it wasn't that Labs were the most perfect specimens or that they could make such long retrieves, or that they could stand the harshest elements that kept people breeding them time and again. Perhaps it was simply that look in those soulful eyes that penetrated everything else and just spoke to humans, thus assuring the Lab's existence and bringing them to where they are today, as our partners, our companions, our friends.

Regardless of the type of Labrador shape and size your dog conforms to, there remains certain characteristics that apply to the Lab across the board. Personality, temperament, and intelligence are three important traits that endear these wonderful dogs to us, their owners; these things make our beloved Labs special.

– Vickie Lamb

Part 2
A Brief History of Labs

You can't know the dogs without knowing their background

by E. Donnall Thomas Jr.

They flush pheasants and fetch ducks, guide the blind and sniff out contraband at border crossings, lick faces and enrich lives. At some point, every Lab enthusiast must wonder about the origins of the remarkable animal that has become the most popular dog in America. In fact, the Lab's history turns out to be laced with enough intrigue to fuel a spy novel, reflecting the difficulties of reconstructing events that took place over three centuries, across one ocean and in two nations divided, as one sage noted, by a common language.

66I recently had a non-hunting Lab owner ask me how anyone could make dogs jump into icy water to fetch a duck. Had she truly understood the breed, she might have asked how anyone could refuse to let them.99

– E. Donnall Thomas Jr.

Archimedes observed that given a fulcrum he could move the world. In similar fashion, unraveling historical mysteries often goes best by starting with an event generally accepted as true, even if that means beginning in

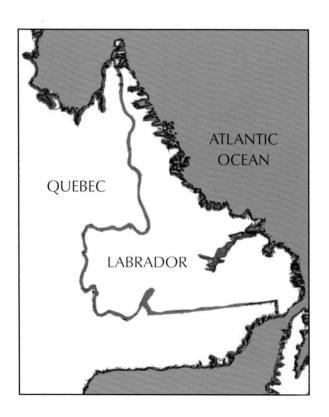

the middle of the story. The British Col. Peter Hawker probably provided the first written description of the Lab in his 1814 treatise *Instructions to Young Sportsmen*. Referring to the St. John's dog in distinction from the larger, more familiar Newfoundland, he wrote: "The other, by far the best for every kind of shooting, is oftener black than of another color, and scarcely bigger than a pointer. He is made rather long in the head and nose; pretty deep in the chest; very fine in the legs; has short smooth hair; does not carry his tail so much curled as the other; and is extremely active in running, swimming..." All of which sounds pretty much like someone we know.

While it's relatively easy to follow the trail forward from the British St. John's dog of the early 19th century to the modern Lab, tracing the Lab's ancestry from the coast of Newfoundland to Hawker's day proves far more involved. Writers, alas, must bear their share of responsibility for the confusion. When the Lab returned to the New World as a popular East Coast sporting breed in the 1900s, commentators created a history to accompany it. In the process, they perpetuated two central ideas: that the Lab derived from the Newfoundland and that the Newfoundland in turn derived from indigenous New World canines. Unfortunately, both ideas are probably untrue.

Abundant evidence confirms that Native Americans lived and hunted with large dogs. But British explorers reached the coast of Newfoundland as

What's in a Name
Some credit the 3rd Earl of Malmesbury (1807-1889) for giving the breed its name of "Labrador retriever," changing it from Little Newfoundlander. Others say that after Edwin Landseer's painting of "Cora," the next time the name "Labrador" showed up was by the 5th Duke of Buccleuch in 1839; he is also credited with having the first kennel of "Labradors" in Scotland.

> *It is important for any Labrador fancier or judge to recognize and appreciate that the Labrador imported into England and introduced into this country... for one, and only one, purpose—to retrieve upland game and waterfowl.*
>
> – Dr. Bernard W. Ziessow

early as 1494, and there is no reliable record of dogs in the area until British fishermen arrived two centuries later. The romantic notion that our Labs' genes originated here in North America enjoys little objective support. On the contrary, the breed's ancestors almost certainly crossed the Atlantic as working dogs employed by Devon fishermen plying their dangerous trade along Newfoundland's rugged coast.

As for the derivation of the Lab (then known as the St. John's dog) from the Newfoundland, the late Richard Wolters has done a brilliant job of proving it was probably the other way around. In the face of sketchy direct evidence, Wolters

The Lab's ancestors were originally used to help fishermen along Newfoundland's coast fetch lines, nets, and fish.

argued that the dog's original job description favored the smaller breed, which had to crowd into cramped dories while waiting for a chance to fetch lines, nets, and fish for its masters. The appearance of the larger Newfoundland coincided with the later development of permanent settlements along the coast, when colonists needed large, powerful dogs to haul heavy loads of firewood.

And what were the origins of the dog that crossed the Atlantic to the New World in the first place? The most likely candidate for the title of Lab's Ultimate Ancestor is the St. Hubert's hound, originally of French origin but plainly popular in England at the time Newfoundland's first settlers embarked. Definitive answers remain elusive, but both the written description and drawings of this breed in George Turbervile's *Booke of Hunting*, published in 1576, bear a striking resemblance to modern Labs.

By this complex route, the St. John's dog became a popular British sporting breed in the early 1800s, as evidenced by Delabere Blaine's description of the breed in his *Encyclopedia of Rural Sports*, published in 1840. "The St. John's breed is preferred by sportsmen on every account, being smaller, more easily managed and sagacious in the extreme. His scenting powers are also great... Gentlemen have found them so intelligent, so faithful, and so capable of general instruction that they have given

A Dog By Any Other Name

At the core of a Lab beats the heart of a wolf. It is common knowledge that dogs are descendants from wolves (Latin name *Canis lupus*), but until recently, we didn't know how closely they were related. Once known by the Latin name *Canis familiaris*, the domesticated dog was reclassified by the Smithsonian and Society of Mammalogists in 1993 based on the research conducted at UCLA by Dr. Robert Wayne, a canine evolutionary biologist. It's new name? *Canis lupus familiaris*—a subspecies of the wolf, done so based on research that shows wolf DNA and domestic dog DNA as being 99.8 percent identical.

up most sporting varieties and content themselves with these..." And along the way the breed acquired its enduring name when the popular sporting artist Edward Landseer painted *Cora: A Labrador Bitch*, in 1823.

Unfortunately, the Lab's reputation fared better during the 19th century than the dogs themselves. American independence and changes in the fishing trade decreased direct commerce between the breed's point of origin in Newfoundland and the new market for them among the British aristocracy. Attempts to promote a sheep industry in Newfoundland led to new

restrictions on dog rearing there. No matter how highly English sportsmen suddenly valued Labs, they couldn't get enough of them to maintain breeding stock and the breed faced the serious threat of extinction.

But there are no friends like friends in high places, and the Lab was fortunate enough to enjoy the favor of just the right people. During the first half of the 19th century, the 2nd Lord of Malmesbury, the 5th Duke of Buccleuch, and the 10th Earl of Home, all avid sportsmen, established breeding programs and went to considerable lengths to import what fresh breeding stock they could from Newfoundland. All fortunately had children interested in maintaining the family kennels, and while none seemed particularly interested in sharing their bloodlines with anyone but each other, they managed to preserve the Lab during the most precarious period in the dogs' history.

While all modern Labs derive from limited bloodlines developed and maintained by a few aristocratic families, by the beginning of the 20th century Labs had truly started to thrive in England and Scotland. The British Kennel Club officially recognized the breed as distinct in 1903. Labs began attracting serious attention in field trials and bench shows, and Viscount Knutsford and Lorna Countess Howe established the Labrador Club in 1916. Back from the brink in England, it was time for the breed to realize the next formative step in its development, which it did by crossing the Atlantic once again.

Charles Meyer registered the first Labrador retriever with the American Kennel Club in 1917. Because American wingshooters of the day approached the field so differently than their staid British counterparts, they viewed their sporting dogs differently as well. They taught their pointers and setters to retrieve as a matter of course, leaving no defined job description for the pure retriever in the pursuit of upland game. Chesapeake Bay retrievers handled the serious work in the water. The Rodney Dangerfields of the sporting world, retrievers didn't enjoy a lot of respect. As late as 1927 there were fewer than thirty retrievers registered with the AKC, all—Labs, Chessies, Goldens, Flat Coated and Curly Coated—lumped together under the single category of "Retrievers."

In characteristics fashion, the amiable Lab—backed by a new generation of enthusiastic American admirers—

Retrieving Basics

Though Labs come with an innate desire to retrieve, you'll need to start honing that desire right away. The best place to begin early lessons is in a hallway in the house. Sit at the open end of the hallway and toss a sock, glove, or small ball for the puppy. With the doors to the rooms closed, your pup will have no place to go except back to you. He'll probably try to race by you, but just gather him up in your arms, praise him while he holds the object, and then gently separate him from the object, tossing it again. He'll soon learn that the quicker he runs back to you and gives up the object, the longer the game continues. Just make sure to keep it fun and stop with him wanting more!

"She fetched it. Let her read it."

And The Winner is...

The first American field event held for the breed by the Labrador Retriever Club took place in 1931 in New York. Carl of Boghurst, a yellow Lab, beat out kennelmate Odds On, a black Lab, and captured the Open All-Age stake.

set about changing all that. Initially, the Lab's reputation as a favorite of the British aristocracy helped fuel the breed's popularity among America's status conscious *nouveau riche*, the social class to which most early Lab importers belonged. But it was only a matters of time until the breed's reputation began to disseminate to the general sporting public, largely as the result of the dogs' performance in field trials. The new American Labrador Retriever Club held the breed's first trial in 1931. Although the tests were hardly demanding by today's standards, the event drew considerable attention. By the end of the decade, Lab trials had become popular, well-publicized events attended by amateur handlers as well as the professionals who originally managed dogs for their wealthy owners.

The history of the Lab's development as a field trial star during the middle of the last century is well documented. Meanwhile, to considerably less fanfare, other events were taking place that in my opinion contributed just as much to the breed's eventual development into the Lab we know today. Introduced to Oregon in the 1880s, the ring-necked pheasant expanded its range across the Midwest, attracting a major following among everyday sportsmen in the process. In contrast to the quail, wood-cock and grouse that defined the upland gun dog's original American job description, pheasants favored heavy cover, ran relentlessly before flushing, and proved exceptionally difficult to

Lab Stamp

King Buck—a famous field dog handled by a famous trainer (Cotton Pershall) and owned by a famous kennel (John Olin's Nilo Farms)—won the National Open Retriever Championship in 1952 and 1953. But he is perhaps more famous for being the only dog ever to appear on the Federal Waterfowl Stamp. He was painted by Maynard Reece for the 1959 stamp, which is required by all waterfowl hunters in the nation.

recover after the shot. The explosion of interest in outdoor sports that followed the end of the Second World War found American upland hunters in sore need of a new type of gun dog that could beat the wily ringneck at its own game. The demands of pheasant hunting practically defined the previously unknown concept of the flushing retriever, and the Lab proved ideally suited to fill this complex new job description.

And as Labs replaced Chessies in the duck blind and pointers in the field, a subtle change took place in the everyday relationship between the dogs and their owners. In 19th century Britain and even during the early years of the Lab's introduction to American, sporting dogs largely existed to entertain the rich. Cared for by servants and trained by professional handlers, Labs of that era enjoyed a distant, largely impersonal relationship with those who owned them and determined the future of the breed. But as Labs grew more versatile in the field, they became popular among Americans of all walks of life. Rather than retiring automatically to the kennel at the end of the day, they rode around in trucks, lounged in front of fireplaces, and played with kids. In short, they became family dogs, and the personality traits that suited their new role in life became as highly regarded as the courage and tenacity that had made them popular in the field.

"I TOLD you labs were great with kids."

Every canine, no matter the breed, was bred and developed to fulfill a role for humans, even if that role was nothing more than for companionship. But, because of their intelligence, trainability, and willingness to please, perhaps

Part 3
Punching the Clock

"Labs have always had jobs to do, jobs that require specific skills and hard-wired behaviors but that also require an unusual capacity to adapt and respond creatively."

– Tom Davis

no other breed has found more willing employers in such a wide variety of fields than the Lab. While Labs started out as hunting dogs, their unique and valuable traits have made them impressive athletes, important and useful service dogs, and irreplaceable companions to millions.

The Athlete

Their fishing excursions aside, the earliest days of the Lab are highlighted by its ability as both a waterfowl and upland hunter. Their prowess in the outdoors is what kept the breed from extinction in the first place, so it's only fitting that, in any listing of the different job Labs perform, that hunting occupies the top spot.

The Lab's ability to retrieve, their desire to find and flush game, and their companionship with their human partners in the field are the essence of this breed. No water is too cold, no cover is too thick, and no game is too tough for a Lab. It isn't surprising, then, that the earliest competitions designed to test the dogs—and thereby which ones would get chosen for breedings for the development of blood-

Not only are Labs America's most popular dog, they are also the hunting community's favored canine for waterfowl and upland gamebird hunting.

lines and the betterment of the breed as a whole—were mock hunting situations. However, the first field trial events were social events, as well, and, since the sport (and the dogs) were brought over from England, a touch of the aristocracy and romance of the kingdom came with it. Those early field trial reports read like a Manhattan dinner party.

As time went on, though, two things began happening, both of which had a tremendous impact on the sort of field events. First, more retriever clubs popped up all around the country, opening up the possibility for anyone to get involved, and second, the field trials themselves—because the dogs competing were coming from more refined breedings and were brilliant in their ability to achieve tremendous field feats—became more difficult and the judging more particular. The tests themselves began to represent nothing that a dog might encounter during a regular hunting situation, with retrieves hundreds of yards long and only slight faults disqualifying dogs (but such difficult tasks were necessary in order to separate winners from the rest of the field).

As such, other contests came into existence, most notably what are called hunt tests—sponsored by the American Kennel Club, United Kennel Club, and North American Hunting Retriever Association (NAHRA)—providing a place for the average hunter to take his dog during the off-season to get in some more refined training—and lots of experience and exercise. Dogs competing in

"No no! Not HERE!
Wait till you're closer to THEM!"

Retriever Basics

Though you will more than likely teach your Lab the common commands of "sit," "stay," "come," "heel," "kennel," "fetch," and "down," you may want to get creative and see how far you can expand your dog's vocabulary. Here are a few other useful commands: "hurry-up" (to get the dog to go to the bathroom on command, great when you're at a rest area while on a trip); "drink" (to get your dog to take a drink, also useful while on a trip); and "shake" (not to shake your hand, but to shake the water off after coming out of the lake—it allows you to step away from the dog).

these tests are not judged against one another but against a set standard—in other words, it is possible for every dog in the trial to attain the top honors and titles. These tests more closely approximate what a normal hunting dog could expect to see during a season of hard waterfowl and upland hunting.

The other most popular sport for Labs is in the show ring. This might not seem like it fits under "The Athlete" category, but training and competing for conformation events can be intense. Labs need to adhere particularly well to the breed standard to achieve show titles, as well as learn how to behave in the arena—with all of the other people and dogs around, impeccable manners are necessary—and how to properly stand for inspec-

Best in Show

Since it started handing out "Best In Show" awards in 1907, the Westminster Kennel Club Dog Show—perhaps the most recognized bench show in the country—has never seen a Lab awarded the top honor. As surprising as that fact is, it might be more surprising to learn that since 1924, when the Club began awarding individual group honors (based on the AKC groups the breed belongs to; in the Lab's case, the "Sporting" group), no Lab has even claimed the top spot in Best In Group. The best Labs have done? Four seconds, and four fourths in Best In Group. The first time a Lab placed, it took a second in 1933.

THE CRAP I PUT UP WITH FOR A LOUSY BOWL OF KIBBLES...

COCHRAN!

Dog Titles

Some of the titles associated with conformation and obedience competitions are: CH (Champion); OTCH (Obedience Trial Champion); CD (Companion Dog); CDX (Companion Dog Excellent); TD (Tracking Dog); TDX (Tracking Dog Excellent); UDT (Utility Dog); UDTX (Utility Dog Excellent); CGC (Canine Good Citizen).

tion and trot around the ring. One of the primary benefits for people with show dogs is the value that is added to their dogs with titles, which can be used to command higher prices for puppies or stud fees.

In obedience competitions, a Lab's skills are put to the test to see if he or she is a "good citizen" in any setting and with any person. Some of the tasks the dog is asked to do are to maintain a proper heeling position, long sits and stays, extended time spent in a down position, retrieves over obstacles, scent discrimination, and even tracking. Some obedience competitions have even started to toss some agility skills into the mix. Dogs with advanced obedience titles have proven themselves as highly intelligent, well-mannered, and dependable individuals. For the person who wants a dog simply to be a well-rounded family companion, training for an obedience competition teaches excellent skills.

A Lab's athletic ability shines brightest, perhaps, in the frenetic sport of agility. Jumping over bars, racing up wooden frames, scrambling through shoots, zigzagging between poles, all in an effort to complete a course in the fastest time with the least number of faults... it's enough to make the casual observer dizzy—and the participants addicted. There may be other dog sports to watch, but none may be more fun. Some of the obstacles the dogs navigate are the A-frame; dog walk; seesaw; tunnels; the weave poles; single-, double-, and triple-bar jumps; tire jumps; and many more. Be very, very

careful about starting agility—if you have the right kind of Lab with the right attitude, you won't want to quit.

One of the newer Lab games on the scene is Big Air (the dog long jump), which might be stealing the show, especially since it is a dog event that is so easily televised and such a crowd pleaser. It is arguably the most popular event at ESPN's "Great Outdoor Games" every summer. As their handler tosses a favorite object high into the air, these dogs race down a dock and jump off into a portable, deep pool. Sounds simple and it can be, provided the Lab has the right training and the notion that he's got wings. Right now, the world record for the dog long jump is held by a spastic black Lab named Little Morgan: 26 feet, 6 inches.

All Labs love to retrieve, especially in water.

❝When you watch good Labs work, you
get the sense that they are muttering
under their breath, 'If only I could fly...
if only I could fly... if only...'**❞**

– Steve Smith

In flyball, perhaps the only "team" event, dogs (of any breed) race toward a spring-loaded box, leaping four hurdles along the way. When they get to the box, the dog is trained to step on it, at which point a ball pops out. The dog fetches it, races back across the

hurdles to the starting line, and the next dog is sent. In this relay race, four dogs and handlers make up a team.

Dogs have a natural inclination to pull, and in skijoring, this is put to good use. Using a harness around the dog's shoulders that is attached to a person's belt, the dog mushes while the person cross-country skis. Talk about getting in shape!

A Lab is not really a Lab if he hasn't at least been tossed a Frisbee to catch. For those that show a knack for snatching disks out of the air, the possibilities are endless for what you can teach your dog, and there are competitions, demonstrations, and clubs to get you involved.

The Good Samaritan

While Labs were originally developed to aid hunters, their intelligence and calm temperament (with the right training) have allowed them to be used in a multitude of service roles for humans. More important than titles and ribbons, service dogs save lives, stop criminals, redefine a person's existence, and simply brighten days. Today, Labs have replaced every other breed in almost every service role in which aggression is not necessary (such as a police attack dog).

A fun skill to teach your Lab—and necessary if he is to be a hunter or competitor, but also fun for the yard—is that of "handling," in which your Lab follows your hand signals to find the object to be fetched. When combined with a "whistle-sit," you can use commands such as "back," "over," and "in," to handle your dog to his goal.

Perhaps the best known service dogs are the guide dogs, those that, when attached to a harness, lead a visually impaired or blind person into the world. It is uncanny what these dogs know and how they react to certain situations, and it's wonderful that these people can put their entire trust in their four-legged guides. Breeding programs and training is very specialized, and organizations across the country are always looking for more dogs and financial support.

As handicap-assistance dogs, Labs bring a sense of wholeness to someone who may have otherwise never known it. Everything from fetching dropped pencils, turning on light switches, picking up the phone and fetching it to the owner, and holding

open a department store door are per-
formed by these dogs. These specially
trained Labs free people from the con-
strictions placed on them by wheel-
chairs or mental incapacitations.

The Lab's extreme
sense of smell is put to
use in many different
ways. Search-and-rescue
Labs traverse natural and
manmade disaster areas in
search of survivors or
human remains, and scent
trackers comb mountain-
sides or wilderness tracts
looking for lost individuals.
Labs have even been
trained to detect human
scent under water, with
the dogs traveling up and

down rivers or across lakes in a boat, their heads over the edge.

For police, military, and customs officers, Labs are used to detect drugs, bombs, and other contraband in a multitude of settings. In this world's current environment, with a heightened fear of terrorist attacks, much of our safety can be traced to a Lab's nose giving it the "A-OK," either in a plane, train, subway, or airport. K-9 units in police departments across the country rely on their furry officers to detect narcotics on suspects, in vehicles, or in buildings (a dog's find of drugs is considered practically unimpeachable in a court of law). Fire departments also use Labs to detect the cause of a fire to see if arson is to blame for a blaze.

The sweet disposition of the Labrador retriever makes it one of the most popular breeds in the arena of therapy work, a service role that, unlike the others, anyone can involve their dog. Simply by visiting the elderly, sick, and shut-in, performing a few tricks or lending an ear to be scratched—or whispered into—Labs cheer up many people and give a breath of fresh air in an otherwise bleak day.

The Companion

Perhaps your Lab is not destined for an icy duck blind or the winner's circle; maybe she won't weave through poles or soar off a dock on ESPN; he

"They do have a tendency to become part of the family, don't they?"

might not even bring laughter to a children's cancer ward or thwart a drug-smuggling operation. No matter, for the dog will be quite happy fulfilling all of those roles—though on a much smaller scale and with a much smaller audience—right in your own family.

Labs will lick tears and bring smiles after scraped knees, they'll set off in hiking and backpacking adventures all the way across the backyard, they'll jump into kiddie pools and be applauded all the same, they'll fetch a "shot" tennis ball as if it were the biggest goose a young boy had ever seen, and they'll duck and dodge the most frenzied game of tag that a group of eight-year-olds can put together. And at night, they'll snooze away on beds or couches or in front of

the fire, keeping an ear tuned to the
normal creaks and groans of
the house and its occu-
pants, ever vigilant for
something out of the
ordinary that just might
need a perfunctory sniff,
a causal woof of warn-
ing, or a sympathetic,
furry shoulder to cry on.
Their companionship is
worth more than any
ribbon or flashbulb or
write-up in the local
paper. Almost every Lab
will never shine on TV, but
our lives would not be
complete without them.

As wonderful as the Labrador retriever is, the breed is not without its share of health problems. Their popularity means that there are some unscrupulous breeders who hope

Part 4
What Plagues a Lab

" The capacity of the older Lab to face challenges in the field with enthusiasm and courage never ceases to inspire, and sometimes it can positively break your heart. "

-E. Donnall Thomas Jr.

to make a quick buck, which in turn contributes to the continuation of some of the genetic problems inherent in Labs and most other large dog breeds. The athletic, devil-may-care attitude of the dog itself, plus their affinity for using their mouth on every-

thing, gets them into quite a bit of trouble, too. Reputable breeders take great responsibility in making sure that the prospective parents are free of genetic defects; from there, it's up to the owner to take care of the rest.

Diseases and Genetic Problems

Perhaps the number one genetic problem most associated with Labs—or at least, the one most often thought of when you think of a Lab—is that of canine hip dysplasia (CHD). A malformation of the hip ball-and-socket joint, CHD leads to a dog with near constant pain in the rear legs (unless properly medicated).

Pedigree

Health clearances, particularly for hips and eyes, can be found right on a dog's pedigree. Hips from the OFA are rated as "fair," "good," or "excellent." The dog's age when the X-ray was taken, a certification number and rating, and sex are also recorded. An OFA clearance might read as: LR46113G36M. This translates to: Labrador retriever, certification number 46113, rating of "good," X-rays taken when dog was 36 months of age, and it's a male.

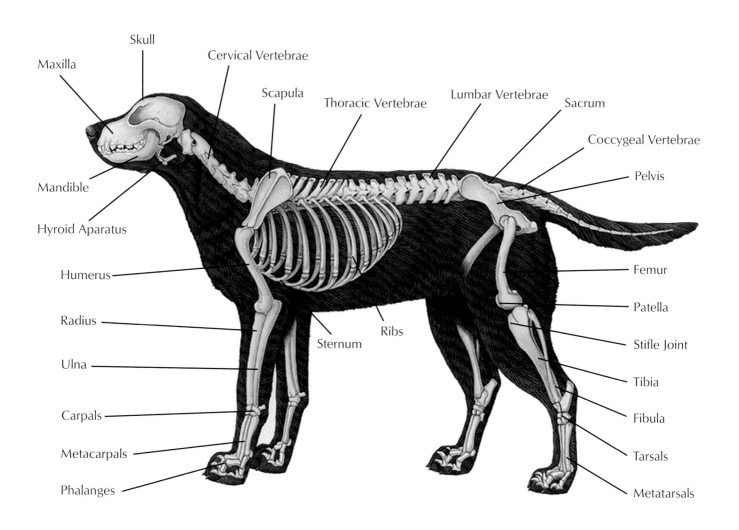

Skull

Maxilla

Cervical Vertebrae

Scapula

Thoracic Vertebrae

Lumbar Vertebrae

Sacrum

Coccygeal Vertebrae

Pelvis

Mandible

Hyroid Aparatus

Humerus

Radius

Ulna

Carpals

Metacarpals

Phalanges

Sternum

Ribs

Femur

Patella

Stifle Joint

Tibia

Fibula

Tarsals

Metatarsals

When it comes to canine hip dysplasia, where does the Lab rank? According to the Orthopedic Foundation for Animals, Labs rate Number 72 (12.4%) in incidence of CHD. This data is based on evaluations from 1974-2004.

The simple fact that Labs are large dogs that are incredibly active leads
to many of their health problems, especially in their legs and knees.

Vigorous work is curtailed, and it may come to a point where even rising from a prone position is difficult; sadly, a Lab's lifespan is often shortened as well. The genetic disease is passed on from the parents who either have CHD or are carriers of the disease. All prospective parents should have their hips examined

either through the Orthopedic

Foundation for Animals (OFA, which

examines hip X-rays for malformations)

or the Pennsylvania Hip Improvement

Program (PennHIP, which performs a test

and X-rays to measure the hip joint's

laxity). These two groups, while evaluat-

ing different aspects of a dog's hips, are

Progressive retinal atrophy (PRA) is a degeneration of the retina that usually develops between three and six years of age.

the gold standard in determining whether or not a dog has CHD. Breeders usually have a copy of the dog's X-rays on hand, too, and though you may not be an expert radiologist, spotting the abnormalities in a CHD X-ray is, unfortunately, pretty easy.

An affliction of the eyes called progressive retinal atrophy (PRA) is another problem that Labs can inherit. Unlike hip dysplasia, PRA is painless, and this degeneration of the retina that develops over time and eventually causes blindness, usually pops up between three and six years of age. The Canine Eye Registry Foundation (CERF) screens dogs and parents for eye problems, and these clearances, like those for hip dysplasia, can be found on the pedigree.

Centronuclear myopathy (formerly called Labrador retriever myopathy) is a new problem that has many owners of Labs, particularly those from field trial bloodlines, pretty scared. This genetic malady impairs the individual muscle fibers that are responsible for fast, explosive movement, leaving those fibers in charge of slower, longer-duration motion to handle everything. The result is a lame Lab that tires very easily. Treatment is still in its infancy, but it appears that, with the right amount and kind of care and medication, Labs with this myopathy can go on to live relatively normal lives.

As with any being—human or canine—cancer is of paramount concern, and Labs are not immune to this killer that does not care what breed

you are or how many legs you walk on. Most all of the same cancers that plague humans afflict Labs, and, likewise, many of the treatments are the same—chemotherapy, tumor removal, etc. Sadly, canine cancers seem to progress faster than in humans, and many dogs that develop the disease are usually put to rest rather than forced to endure treatment that might only serve to prolong the agony. It is at these times that we must evaluate our relationship with our beloved friends and make the choice that is appropriate for them, and not base it on our own selfishness.

Other things that can afflict Labs include: tricuspid valve dysplasia (a genetic disease in the heart); allergies (to food, mostly, but some dogs can be

"They do love water, don't they?"

prone to anything); epilepsy (which leads to seizures); thyroid problems (which can contribute to obesity); and a variety of lumps and tumors that are not cancerous but can cause problems with appearance and mobility (most are removed fairly easily with a veterinarian's care).

Bumps and Bruises, Aches & Pains

As with any athlete, sometimes Labs are their own worst enemy. The never-quit drive bred for over generations can cause some focused Labs to get themselves into deep trouble, and it isn't surprising that many of these problems occur in the legs and knees.

Cruciate ligament injuries are extremely common in the hunting and competitive Lab. The repeated pounding and shock to the joints, not to mention traumatic incidents such as stepping in a hole, can eventually lead to a tearing of the ligaments in the rear legs. There are canine orthopedic surgeons who make a pretty good living repairing—or replacing—Labrador retriever knees, and though the dog may never soar as high or run as fast after the injury and treatment, they will still have that drive. It is up to the owners to make sure that, once again, the dog's heart doesn't get ahead of its head.

Though a dog may not actually tear a ligament or blow out a knee, most athletic Labs will, at some point in their lives, be forced to deal with arthritis. Treated through a variety of methods—medication, massage, acupuncture, implants of gold beads, hydrotherapy, and homeopathic alternatives to name a few—arthritis is just one of those things that happens to all old dogs, especially old athletes. Through a modification of diet to keep them thin, nutritional supplements, and making sure they are comfortable, in association with some of the aforementioned methods, arthritis is completely manageable.

You may have heard not to let your dog run too much or too hard very soon after eating, that "their stomach will flip over." While this problem is a very real concern—gastric dilatation volvulus (GDV)—research suggests that it is not caused by sudden exercise on a full stomach. Some dogs and breeds are just prone to it, and Labs—with their deep chests, voracious appetite, and "scarfing" behavior—are one of those breeds. In an incident of GDV, air becomes trapped in the stomach, causing it to "float" out of position and twist, leading to nearly immediate shock, and emergency assistance is critical.

Other "environmental" troubles associated with Labs include tooth and ear problems

"Shot time again?"

First Aid Kit

A first-aid kit for your Lab should include, at the very minimum, the following: your veterinarian's office and emergency number (programmed into your cell phone); bandages (Ace, gauze, self-adhesive, etc.); tweezers; gauze sponges; adhesive/athletic tape; forceps; scissors; styptic pencil; triple antibiotic ointment; pliers; saline solution; ear cleaning solution; Betadine; cotton swabs, buffered aspirin (no ibuprofen), Benadryl, and current medications your dog is taking. Ask your vet to help you make up a kit.

(particularly ear infections due to trapped water); obesity; heat stroke (extremely common, deadly, and easy to avoid if you pay attention); and typical bumps, bruises, and scrapes from leading an active lifestyle. Many of these types of things can be treated with the help of a good home veterinary manual and a well-stocked first aid kit.

The Dangers of Home

Just as a home should be baby-proofed before the arrival of a new infant, so must it be "Lab-proofed." The home is one of the primary sources of dangers for Labs, and with this breed being such a people-dog, vigilance is a requirement for the Lab owner. All of the dangers a Lab can get into around the house are preventable and caused by negligence (and accidents can happen fast with an energetic Lab, especially a puppy).

It's common knowledge that the theobromine in chocolate is toxic to dogs (baker's chocolate and cacao beans are the worst), but it's now been shown that grapes, onions, and raisins can even be harmful. There are a variety of toxic house and garden plants, and Labs love to graze.

Poisons for rats, slugs, mice, and other rodents can also be just as deadly for a Lab. Antifreeze may be one of the number one killers of dogs around the house, for the sweet smell and taste can lure a scavenging Lab. Only a few laps can be enough to kill even a big dog, so most pet-owning homes have switched to brands of

You really can't go wrong if you feed your Lab a quality dry dog food for the different stages in his life—puppy, adult, senior, etc. Follow the guidelines printed right on the bag, for they have been tailored to the protein, fat, and other ingredients in that food. Some of the strictest scientific testing goes on in the halls and kennels of major pet food manufacturers, with the test subjects getting cared for as well as most family dogs and going to good homes after a test is completed.

antifreeze that tout their "pet friendliness." (This doesn't mean, however, that you can let them loose in the garage, but some of the risk is gone.) Lawn chemicals, household cleaning supplies, fertilizers... pretty much anything you wouldn't let your child touch, your Lab shouldn't come in contact with either.

The trash barrel might be the one place that is the most dangerous, for it has the potential to contain nearly all of the above items. Barrels and cans with secure lids are a necessity, as is not leaving a plate full of chicken scraps and bones, with their delightful aroma wafting through the house, just underneath the lid. A Lab will invent a way to get into that kind of can.

While in town, it's always best to keep your dog on a leash.

Chew on this...

With Labs doing so much for us by way of their mouths, it's no secret that their mouths are going to get them into trouble. You'll want to have lots of different chew toys around to save your furniture legs, shoes, hats, and other, more deadly items that a roaming, bored, destructive chewer can find.

Labs like to chew, obviously, but they also like to consume. Bowel obstructions are very common in this breed, and some veterinarians have had some pretty strange things show up on X-rays. These obstructions are no laughing matter, however, because they can kill a dog. Children's toys, socks, pantyhose, coins, rocks, batteries... you name it, and some Lab somewhere has tried to swallow it.

Finally, the number one danger around the house is what runs outside of it: the road. Exuberant Labs enjoying a game of fetch, chasing a Frisbee, or taking off after an especially bothersome squirrel do not look ahead to see the car that just turned down the street. Too many Labs are claimed every year because they were so focused on something else that they couldn't hear commands to stop, or they were simply allowed to roam free because, "Oh, he'll stick around the yard." Labs are, at their core, hunters, and hunters are explorers, and they will roam in search of fun and game if given the opportunity. Fence in the yard, get an electronic fence, train him to stop instantly on command, or otherwise have some way of keeping in contact with the dog, and don't let your eye stray.

The average lifespan of a Labrador retriever is around 12 years. That is much too short a time as it is and, regrettably, there are some things that will make our time together even shorter. Thankfully, Labs are such revelers in life that even if something

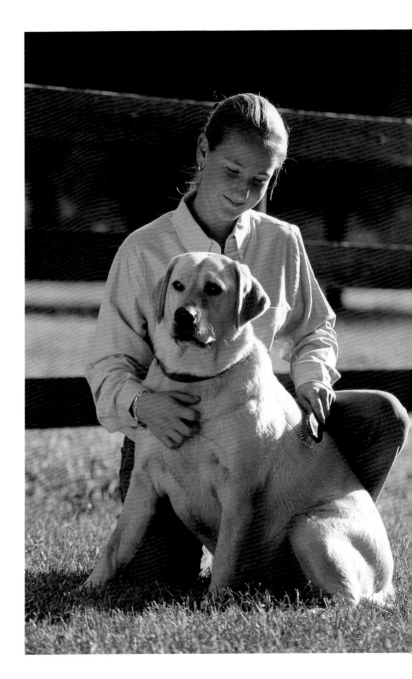

tragic happens or develops, they will pack as much as possible into what time they do have, and the impact on our lives will not be measured by how long they are with us. Whether we lose a puppy because of an awful accident or wake to find that an old timer has drifted away in his sleep, Labs wrap us around their paws from that first moment we lean over the box and make contact with those eyes so full of life, so full of energy, so full of wisdom. It is the one great injustice in life that dogs live so short a life, but it does mean that we get to love that many more.

Helpful Information

Orthopedic Foundation for Animals
2300 E. Nifong Blvd.
Columbia, MO 65201
(573) 442-0418
ofa@offa.org
www.offa.org

Canine Eye Registry Foundation
625 Harrison St.
Purdue University
W Lafayette, IN 47907
(765) 494-8179
CERF@vmdb.org
www.vmdb.org/cerf.html

PennHIP (Pennsylvania Hip Improvement Program)
University of Pennsylvania
3900 Delancey St.
Philadelphia, PA 19104
(215) 573-3176
pennhipinfo@pennhip.org
www.pennhip.org

National Retriever Club, Inc.
15174 Channel Dr.
Laconner, WA 98257
www.working-retriever.com/nrc/index.html

The Labrador Retriever Club of America
P.O. Box 9
Clipper Mills, CA 95930-0009
info@thelabradorclub.com
www.thelabradorclub.com

North American Hunting Retriever Association
4353 Charity Neck Rd.
Virginia Beach, VA 23457-1525
jvandergiessen@att.net
www.nahra.org

United Kennel Club
100 E. Kilgore Rd.
Kalamazoo, MI 49002
(269) 343-9020
www.ukcdogs.com

American Kennel Club
260 Madison Ave
New York, NY 10016
(212) 696-8200
www.akc.org

North American Dog Agility Council
11522 South Hwy. 3
Cataldo, ID 83810
info@nadac.com
www.nadac.com

Master National Retriever Club
116 Alta Vista Dr.
Marion, AR 72364
www.masternational.com

Super Retriever Series
www.superretrieverseries.com

Therapy Dogs International
88 Bartley Rd.
Flanders, NJ 07836
(973) 252-7171
tdi@gti.net
www.tdi-dog.org

Guiding Eyes for the Blind
611 Granite Springs Rd.
Yorktown Heights, NY 10598
800-942-0149
www.guidingeyes.org

Canine Companions for Independence
P.O. Box 446
Santa Rosa, CA 95402-0446
(866) 224-3647
www.caninecompanions.org

Guide Dogs for the Blind
P.O. Box 151200
San Rafael, CA 94915
800-295-4050
www.guidedogs.com

National Disaster Search Dog Foundation
206 N. Signal St., Suite R
Ojai, CA 93023
(888) 459-4376
rescue@ndsdf.org
www.searchdogfoundation.org

The Bird Dog Foundation/
Retriever Field Trial Hall of Fame
P.O. Box 774
505 Hwy. 57
Grand Junction, TN 38039
(731) 764-2058
www.birddogfoundation.com

Photo Credits